This is your guide to plurals.
Which means more than one of something.

A is for Apple. So more than one Apple is………

Apples

B is for is for Branch. So more than one Branch is.........

Branches

C is for Car.
So more than one Car is.........

Cars

D is for Dog.
So more than one Dog is..........

Dogs

E is for Egg.
So more than one Egg is.........

Eggs

F is for Fish.
So more than one
Fish is.........

Fishes

G is for Goat.
So more than one
Goat is.........

Goats

H is for House.
So more than one
House is..........

Houses

I is for Icon.
So more than one
Icon is.........

Icons

J is for Juice.
So more than one Juice is.........

Juices

K is for Key.
So more than one Key is.........

Keys

L is for Leaf.
So more than one
Leaf is……..

Leaves

M is for Mountain. So more than one Mountain is……..

Mountains

N is for Nut.
So more than one Nut is..........

Nuts

O is for Orange. So more than one Orange is..........

Oranges

P is for Pear.
So more than one Pear is.........

Pears

Q is for Quince. So more than one Quince is........

Quinces

R is for Radish.
So more than one
Radish is.........

Radishes

S is for Sock.
So more than one Sock is..........

Socks

T is for Tree.
So more than one
Tree is……...

Trees

U is for Umbrella. So more than one Umbrella is.........

Umbrellas

V is for Vulture. So more than one Vulture is.........

Vultures

W is for Window. So more than one Window is..........

Windows

X is for Xylophone. So more than one Xylophone is………

Xylophones

Y is for Yam.
So more than one
Yam is.........

Yams

Z is for Zebra.
So more than one Zebra is.........

Zebras